THE LIGHT IN THEM
IS PERMANENT

THE LIGHT IN THEM IS PERMANENT

ॐ

99 Sonnets by
STEVEN NIGHTINGALE

RAINSHADOW EDITIONS
THE BLACK ROCK PRESS
2010

Cloth Edition:
ISBN: 978-1-891033-47-6

Trade Paper Edition:

ISBN 978-1-891033-49-0

Library of Congress Control Number: 2010924137

The Black Rock Press
University of Nevada, Reno Reno, NV 89557-0044
www.blackrockpress.org
Printed in the United States of America

Cover Image:
Le Lecteur. Provenant d'Iran. 16th century.
Scala Archives.

For Lucia and Gabriella
  —mi destino, mi delectación, mi paz

Contents

Introduction

L ET US TAKE AN ORDINARY DAY, an ordinary moment—say, your little daughter opens a door and walks into the room where you are working. With her comes the afternoon light, and warm air with the fragrance of oak and sage. She stands before you in grass-stained jeans. Blue flower petals cling to her shirt. She shows the uncanny grace and blessed energy natural to any child. You rise, and go to her; down on your knees you gather her into your arms, in wonder at her fierce, soft beauty.

Any parent anywhere in the world may have just such an encounter. Within it there is strange, open, wild country: the country between a moment of life, and what it means. It is just one moment, yet its meaning makes a light we can live by.

To venture into that wild country, in hopes of understanding, we need help. Poetry is here to help. It is our helpmate, our provisions, our surety; it gives us the forms in which we may hold meaning, all in the name of what we love, in devotion to those we love. It's our chance to gather, concentrate, and clarify experience, so as to give it away into other hands, in hopes that it may be accepted, that it may be of service.

For me, the form is the sonnet. For over twenty-five years, it has been my guide into the wilderness of daily life. I have returned from my adventures safely, so far, not because of any virtues of my own, but because in my traveling through the magical, hazardous lands where I live—where we live—the sonnet has been so trustworthy a companion.

Whatever our suffering, most of us know that here on earth we will come round to days and nights of irresistible beauty. We will have our chance to give thanks, to learn, to love the little girl coming into the room; to praise and cherish our mate, to offer all we have to our friends. And we will have the sacred chance to love strangers.

You, reader, are a stranger to me. These sonnets are written for you, and though I may be a wandering, worn, idiosyncratic man, I pray you might be willing to take this book in hand.

It is the simplest fact of this labor: I write with all I have and hope, and I write for you. You are present to me, always. I think of you, your powers and generosity, your hardships, your searching, your openheartedness. Only in your hands, does a book count for anything. Only by your understanding, does beauty come fully alive. Only by your good will and good work, will history be answered and darkness undone.

—S.N.
Big Sur, April 2009

The Reader as Bright-Souled Beauty

A doorway: built of fourteen lines,
An order beyond, of sacred designs

For you and me, our future and past,
Our music, sweat, story, devotion,
Spring rain, whiskey—everything, cast

From the light that is in you. We pray
To live there, and here: on this earth
Of our rejoicing. If I can die, and obey,
Learning with you what light is worth,

We will open this door. I may fail you—
One syllable wrong, and I lose the sun.
I have come here to sing, to love you,

This is how I live: here in your hands—
Bright-souled beauty, who understands.

Who Said, Who Decided, Who?

Who decided, say, that the iguana's crest
Is better on a lizard, than on the chest

Of a banker? That wings of flamingoes
Should not be lent to children, for soaring
Around the neighborhood; that ice floes

Should not ride the ocean of sand dunes,
With cool mist for a caravan of pilgrims
Golden with heat? Who said that tunes
On a cheap radio, old plastic hairpins,

A soiled deck of cards, book of matches—
The common, plain, are not now restoring
By force of humility, the trust the catches

Every kindling soul with paradisiacal fire?
Who said your real voice is not the choir?

Assorted Questions and Answers in a Man

You think the body goes of itself?
That the brain is a commonwealth

Where the animal we are is exalted,
Where we work enslaved to survival,
Arabesque of electrons, bodies vaulted

In biochemical triumph—old celebration
By material of itself. It could be so.
We may be composed only of sensation.
What you think, may be what you know.

Unless real work is to make by hand
The moonlight. Unless liberty, archival
Honey of souls, daisy, dawn, and sand

Are one story, and to earth we were sent—
Except for heaven, there is no movement.

It's a Job, and Just Happens To Be Our Job

Touch world anywhere, it turns into beauty.
Put forth your hand: a prophecy, a unity

Is plain, is phosphor, at work on earth,
Hidden in dust-mote, mustard-seed,
Luck and kindling of light from birth

Beyond death, to a beginning that is
The future. Can you juggle our months
High into a home in the jetstream? Give
A party with stars and wind? Watch stunts

Of coyotes, mustang, the smooth arc
Of wild rivers, as with cosmic ease
A baby sucks honey off your finger? A spark

You bear, means you are a messenger.
What is given, you and sunlight deliver.

Gates

Because a snowflake shines in the sun, it
Can become the sun—its gleaming a wit

Inside life, saying: each crystal come
From the sky at midwinter, still is going
Home. Love, our minutes make a sum.

Sandhill cranes in high formation spell
Your name; morning light moving through
The beautiful grass turns around to tell
A story; the hours join hands and renew

A rhythm that spins a planet that makes
Us, is made by us, only in our knowing
The whole name, story and dance: gates

Open to our labors, when we understand
How we must leave our beloved homeland.

When We Begin

When you do not match your likeness, your
Profile changes like the cloud edge, the shore
You are is formed by the waves you make;
When you stand forth and let wind shake

A soul from your flesh, and wings of vision
You visit on the body of your sight; your days
You rescue in midair, from a gear train driven
By your career in time; you draw your face

Over again, according to prophecy, learn then
Your voice is not yours, that what is drawn
Is death worth having; and that in the song
For one you love you lose your words, when

You are made over, according to love and her lineage,
In the likeness of all the earth, in her moving image.

Sailing With Her into Her Bright World

The tropics, a clipper on the clearing sea,
A world around, bright ring of sympathy;
This is our own ship and our history,
That sails before a wind of fidelity.

We carry legendary kings, lovely tramps,
Liquor made of millenniums; plain lamps,
Witch-cherished, world-traveled, that illumine
The inside of hearts; a pearl-handled lens

For seeing the future. With such cargo,
We travel for home. We live by your care,
Who has sailed us along the roads where
What you have given is what we know.

Sunlight trusts you—roughneck, pole-star—
Where is world, without the world you are?

Asking

Why is it too much to ask, to have
An eschatology of bread? To have

A theology of salt, a divinity school
That teaches how a stag uses horns—
To hold summer high? To have a spool

Of thread your lover may use to sew
The open cuts in heaven; a wooden boat
Whose bow searches the sky, whose rope
Holds story-lines? Our daughters will know

How to lift the sails that catch light.
Is it too much to ask, that spices adorn
The stars; that we taste a birthright

In this bed, my love, finding anew
The comets and cinnamon inside of you?

On Day and Night Observed To Be Amorous

The way the fur of a black cat shines;
Taste of a peach, raspberry vines;

A day warm, supple, ready, coming
Into the arms of the dusk, who loves
Her; in savory darkness their roaming

Has just the languor, this evening, we
Have in bed. Your pleasures I tease
Into first fragrance, original spicery,
Luck and rough gift-giving beauties,

Raucous—O your first pinwheeling
Visitation, a testament, radiant—who loves
You? This man. I see a world cartwheeling

Every day into your loving open arms—
Even light knows your raggedy charms.

Hidden, As The Sun Is Hidden

Believe her—not for what she thought,
But because her soul is built on rock.

What she does and all she says, by spin
Of earth, somersaulting light of dawn,
Make a whole. She can take her pen,

And from cries of birds and buck of wind,
Cracking of cloud, history of lovers who
Awaken whispering; from immortal dolphin
Whose courses in league with light jewel

Letters across the lagoon—from a speaking
In the world, she marks down the song
We must learn, if humiliation and breaking

Of earth is to stop. She is the one to marry—
Transfigured, she pretends to be ordinary.

Say It

Month by month, as words branch, they
Put out leaves of dream, so that one day
Sunlight finds you in flower. What you do
Within those petals, as they give onto

The air, is hold seed; as old friendships
Hold a cluster of stories on a stem
Moist with nectar. Dark perfect tips
Of twigs sketch the new stars, when

Wind moves them. The wind moved you,
Because you planted yourself in traveling,
Because you saw how months were bearing
The flowers you earn; saw then how you

Soar in place. You say what you mean—
In quietness, show the leaves of dream.

Yep, You'll Have to Get Perfect After All

She is transparent: through her a world
Comes in liberty. All sails are unfurled

On her invisible ship, that moves when
She moves, before winds that blow
From beauty, in peace. Her labors wend

A way to hearts, yet are concealed, that
We never know her antics in springtime,
Nor the way, in the stalk of the wildcat,
In meteor showers, in her radiant design

Of story, in woven high-country wildflower,
She works. She knows what you will know.
Her days are seeds. And her blessing of power

As you follow whole light into the future—
You who thought no beauty would endure—

Love in the Great Basin

More than you—dawn energy of a desert
Within you. Not just what I learnt

By your love in a university of light,
But cartwheeling grace, this delectation,
When you call the coolness of night

Into your hands. Not just your beauty,
But scraggly beauty of mustang and coyote,
Dance of mountain in summer minstrelsy,
Meteors studded with opals, and the slope

Of sage like the repose of a loved woman
In the arms of the future: this concentration
Of offerings I have watched, lovely woman,

You compose. I can taste, as you undress,
Salt of soul in the sweetness of your flesh.

Earth and Pain and Life Together

A king here, massacre there; a treaty,
Empire, books, logic, bestiality;

Holy cities, martyrs in certified agony;
Children in song, a polished guillotine;
Lovely ships on a voyage of discovery.

Firestorm of stories, triumphant hearts,
Affidavits and duels, what is it
Worth, the castles, deeds, donkey carts,
What does it measure in scales fit

With day, night; weights of light? Does
The sum mean just what you mean
When you give me your hand? Does

It all rise within our every day of life
The sorrow, beauty, divinity and strife?

A Marriage

There are marriages: say, mountains and spring,
Luscious peace and the longing of a good king,

Salt wind and the braggadocio of sea-birds;
Storm-winds and a comedy of bristlecones,
Golden eagles and this grace: let us learn

My love, to fly. This is our marriage,
Two souls at home, aloft; each one
A wing on love's body, by carriage
Of pleasure lifted to common sky: love

Is a wind from the next world, and pleasure,
My beauty, is the way flesh and bones
Come into delectations of flight. My treasure,

My true love, I need you. Under this cover
You and I marry this world and another.

The Surprising Mechanics of Conception

This word, a silence, touchstone, prayer,
A flower, a torch, and the way her hair

Shows currents of a spring creek, when
Afternoon light leads us to the midmost
Of a season; so all beauties attend

Upon a man and woman in love. When
In soulful animal venturing, they conceive
A child, the easy galaxies arc and wend
In the space of their hopes. A soul leaves

From there to take flesh. They all one day
Will look to stars and remember. A host
Of heaven is present, who in love would stay

With our children, their skylark and heartbeat;
With their work, your trust, this spring heat.

Ultrasound

A filigree of ribs, your hand the size
To hold an orange pip, your head wise

With preternatural lights that bring
All of us here. As your flesh forms,
You do your bright work; you string

Body and heaven on one hope, put
A planet revolving in your touch. You
Make an eyelash, fingernail, a gut—
What is this genius? Beloved child, you

Know paradise has never been lost—
Already you know a work that storms
The soul. In six months, when you cross

Into this world, teach us: in your hands
A pinwheel galaxy, ocean, desert sands.

How She Works, At Six Weeks Old

At dawn I heard three gentle cries,
And rose, and toward our soul's surprise

I went, and stood above the wooden crib.
If I, from black space, were to look down
Upon opalescent earth, and see light bid

Boundless painted life from rock and water,
Within me would move a cyclone of wonder
And thankfulness—yet, that whirling thunder
Would be of small scope, my little daughter,

Set beside the joy of looking at you.
Your peace is rapture. In you, we found
Soul woven through, journey come true.

Riptide of light, homeland in sight—
How you shine as you set heaven right.

Four Months

Of course, she came to mortality. Yet
At four months, all worlds connect

Within her slight form, which has air,
Flame, sand, ocean, all of which
Earth mixes with delectation, to share

This little girl. My love, my daughter,
How is it, when you turn your head
Towards sage, light, meadow, cougar;
When, at morning, we bring you to bed,

And to our whispers you cry out in joy—
How is it that the calloused fist
Of this world opens, the broken toy

Of history is repaired? In you we can see
At last, how paradise has an infancy.

Five Months Old

You arch your back to fit the path
Of your planet around the sun, path

Of a tanager carried by a spring gust,
Path of a beautiful phrase as it moves
In the imagination of history—we trust

Life, my daughter, because of looking
At you. It's the way your every second,
Every cell, is the tip of a bud holding
Plain beauty in world without end,

Because world and you are two names
That mean the same: life that proves
How understanding can undo the chains

On sense, memory, habit, hope. Daughter,
We will undo history and stop the slaughter.

Eighteen Months Old

Is that a daughter, shining, mischievous,
Cartwheeling into the room, sure, rough,

To remind us how heaven is ready?
How your words like packets of light,
Lexicon of grass and galaxies, ecstasy

Of language, come alive in us: we
Hear your soft bright music, we
Remember the open secret; and we
Can learn at last. Why is it a tree

You touched as you took a first step
Grows up to the stars, to give the night
News of you? As you walk you connect

Our world to another. Cyclonic, coy,
Wild filly of wit, jazz-singer of joy.

Two and a Half Years Old

In tapdance of diamonds, beauty moves
From you, like a spring river that cools

All a rancorous world. Life is delicious
Because of you, daughter. I never knew
Such rapids of amusement, rambunctious,

A sweet rough comely spiritous power
Moving through all creation. I never
Knew how girlish mindful power
Could signal all peace. Love, I never

Knew such joy. None of us have. Not
One of us. The world comes true
Because of you. How you live, is what

We trust. We need you, your help.
We need all a world like yourself.

Ventures with a Wooden Spoon

Burn marks in wood that show darkness
Of vinegar, cinnamon; or mindful press

Of buckwheat and nutmeg; olive oil,
Shallots, butter, stock, cream. Every
Day the spoon is ready for rough toil,

Always the center of action, just where
Our labors would see life come together
In careful sacred common measure.
With a homely wooden spoon we share

Old recipes for rapture. Tonight we sit,
Seasoning memory, and come into savory
Concord of earth and soul, ancient wit

Of figs, wheat, nutmeg, honey, salt—
A wooden key opens this treasure vault.

For Jose Luis

You played the clarinet, as our children danced
By candlelight. In them, all an infinite chance

And danger of life, gathered into their steps
As light into a galaxy: among whirling stars
We knew that just then, somewhere, a caress

Undid decades of pain, wounds were healed,
Food delivered, peace dreamed up, prayers
Arced like rainbows, each heart was unsealed
With starlight; and across a meadow, mares

And foals galloped in springtime to a river
Rambunctious with beauty. This night is ours—
Your gift, the gift of our children. The answer

To history is their dancing: nothing can destroy
Their beauty, their loving, their joy, joy. Joy.

You Say Transfiguration Is Required?

You are trustworthy as summertime.
You make soil dream about a grapevine,

Sand about being glass, sound about
Being a song, shadow about being flesh,
Earth about being itself, a garden about

Being paradise. They say the world needs
Statesman, committees, art and bridges.
I say, the world needs you, on the ridges
Of history, where reading and work lead

To flashpoint of transfiguration. Of course,
You say: our days, by learning, may dress
In a handiwork of light. No one is forced

To live as mere flesh, for earthly digestion:
With your loving, answer soul's question.

My Friend, Do This, or That

You must learn. In twilight play a flute
To the moon. Take history's hobnail boot
Out of your heart, teach then the manners
Of the canyons, say how sibylline banners

Of our planet are borne through black space.
Because light will be answered, as we live
This question: arrived here, hearts in place,
Why do we disappoint paradise? In the quiz

And funhouse of careers, heart-cracker
Of cordiality, backslaps in a slaughterhouse,
Biting down daily on cyanide, as we grouse
A way to oblivion? History is a meatpacker.

Be wrapped and marked. Or follow a star
Until the light we see is a world you are.

Do They Matter, Light, Death, and Hope?

Prayer books in a bonfire, pimps in a fight—
Yet, spellbound in backcountry of twilight,
You saw original carnival. Visiting our town,
Hours like acrobats, magicians, clowns,

According to you: by your incantations
We know world at first light. Your work
Is what we know. You bear exaltations
From coyotes, who gather a whole desert

In grace-notes. You hand out in alleyways
Handbills for sideshows: say, midnight mass
In a church of whirlwinds; meadow grass
As hideout for the future; a child who replays

Centuries for revision; the girl whose breath
Holds bright stanzas, a sundance in our death.

She Is a River Guide

The heart has white water; a turbulence
Of heaven, because muscle and conscience

Move and move in the manner of rivers—
We come, love, to a country of wildflowers
And sacraments. Ask then, my life-giver,

Floating high-hearted down canyons, fresh
With bright cascade of hours, wrought
Of one world, then another—what is flesh
But land, water? Through it you run, not

Yourself until, past all turbulence, you
Clear. You bend with delectation. Sour
Pastime and proud mania gone, the true

Rough perfect testimony of the ocean
Calls. You go slow. Rivers are devotion.

The Rain Forest in You at Corcovado

Specialize in light. The rest will follow.
Heaven is steadiness. Use what you know.

Know you are forever with this forest,
And the forest, a perfect book in you.
Around you, leaves open to address

Heaven, they offer the story you are
For the light to read, and all day
You flourish in full shining. You are
That spell of light. Would you obey

The one law of this forest? Everything
You have, you give. Everything you know,
And will know, give. Then, a wing,

Rain, orchid, quetzal, fable, allspice—
Then the summons: life within life.

Paradise and Her Wink of Complicity

Not that we know, but that we
Have a feather of hope—as trustee

Of a classical chance at reality. Worship
Is this: lightning-storm at the crossroads
Of our devotion—look, the wine you tip

Fills the glass forever, if you can taste
What you love. For you are loved, you
Should know: those peppers, the crate
Of rubies, fragrance of lovemaking, view

Of a lapis sea in the lapis afternoon—
None of this would exist. The codes
You learn light stars, power a monsoon,

Bring us the celestial sympathy and fable—
That ordinary news, at the dinner table.

Look Around You, into the Presence

You think light means nothing, that
Only humans are conscious, to pack

True purposes? You crush, win, borrow;
History wearies of you. You will find
You've missed everything, even sorrow.

When spring winds color night sky
And send one leaf from a pear tree
Along the trajectory of blessing, try
To see: it is unity. Stars at liberty

Fall to match that motion, in sympathy,
In joy, in hope. Leaf and star, mind
And moon, storm, joke, cinnamon tree,

Soul of a woman: everything is present.
Not what paradise said. What she meant.

In the Carnival of her Blessing

Lovely cynic, playful cartwheeling songstress
Of the dinner table and classroom, you dress

A world in beautiful ideas. Just standing there
You're a sparkler, a firework darkness loves
And the day needs. You would stand and dare

A mountain lion if he visited, you'd say:
Where among your muscles is the nectary
Of your soul? Love, sit down and stay
Forever and tell your jokes, your story

Of how you tiptoed in a library, and left
The books open and singing, and bear cubs
Licking honey in the lobby. We are bereft

No longer. We open our eyes, crawl,
Walk, then fly to your blessed carnival.

He Examines Himself

What claim have you, to be alive?
Are you honey, or a ransacked hive

Turning to dust as we watch? Are
You a cloud coming to answer hopes
With golden gift-giving rain, or are

You a billow of sand, a man as death,
Holding a beer and a personality. Tell us,
Do you know the truth about the breath
Of that baby—how it moves in trust

Through the skies, with all the winds
Of the world? Do you know which ropes
You can climb to where light begins,

And which fit around your neck? Are
You alive? Dead? Soul, or ruined star?

He Questions Himself

Tell a story, adorn an idea, make
A poem, socialize: yet you can bake

In a roasting pan of yourself, never fear,
Never fear. You write thank-you notes,
Offer the hand of reconciliation, a tear

Of empathy for the grief of a old friend—
What you do will be brought into a light
That shows onto a screen the rough gem
Or the garbage of what you are. Midnight

And noon, sun, moon, sense, work,
Intellect, affect: these are painted cloaks,
Like the body; like time. A clerk

Comes one day, and dismantles this show.
Do you have wings? Are you a sewage flow?

He Confesses To A Stranger

Let me describe this, once and once only.
Paradise is everywhere. Yet I am lonely,

Because of my own evil. I have learned
What expulsion means: being admired
As I am roasted alive. Being turned

On a spit of my own reflections, even as
Winds out of twilight like a mint blessing
Blow over my beloveds. Glowing paths
I walk, are rancid with my own burning,

Fleshly detonation of each day, a firestorm
In each ignorant hour of work. In desire,
At play, a specter—precisely vanishing form

Of a man. If you seek paradise, learn this:
There is no hell: the evil cease to exist.

Thank Heaven Someone Is In Charge

We have a history of consummate killing.
We have been proud, we have been willing.

All the excitement of men is saying who
Dies. It's leadership. Only what they say
Is noble. Nobility is control. It is you,

Prince of the community, who can
Order a random death, doomed birth.
We would not be mere clots of earth,
But be born for you, die on command.

Claim us, murder us, because if not
The terror is too much. We would bray.
We would sicken. Anything. It is our lot

To kill and to kill when they ring the bells.
We will never do anything about ourselves.

Meditating On Whether He Has a Chance

If it can be; if Socrates lives in sagebrush,
If canyons hold a dusk clear and lush,

Mustangs all show iridescent calico—
If what can be, may be, because of a reason
Inside the light, because what we can know

Comes to the meadow and among wildflowers
Turns like a galaxy, in exultation of promises,
In movement that is generosity; if the power
Of learning roams in mischief, to demolish

Me at last, as it must, my love; if I
Cannot be, there is a chance. This season
Of shameful bright ideas: personal sty

Full of piglets. What hope, with this face?
I live in hope to be destroyed by grace.

Now, Let's See, Where Was It?

Heaven was plain to you once, you thought
It looked iridescent, erotic. All you sought

Was there—peaceful, fantastical, amused,
First theater and homely truth. You went
On, wanting to remember, to be schooled,

To labor and love, doing this man's work
And that woman's will, winning and losing,
Searching for grace; in that new book
Finding a phrase we could use as a wing—

As if one wing was good for anything.
Now you say; it must be heaven's moment.
And look around, as you see closing

Doors made of light. You cannot stay
On earth. How did you lose your way?

He Is Virtuous, He Is Glad

What if sunlight is sick of conscience?
Your submission of life as good evidence

In a final court of virtue? Did you think
That morning light is untrustworthy, that
The earth is turning, impeccably, to wink

At itself in a mirror? That a puma searches
A whole mesa, wanting a theatrical chance
To show its graces? That a songbird perches
To stir a honey in himself, and romance

His own hopes? You learned, reflected,
Measured, weighed, judged. What you get
Is a toolbox. Be the one who rejected

The lie. To learn how merely to be good
Is to turn yourself into petrified wood.

Thanks a Lot, Augustine

We stay on message—billboard elegance
Of ideas, cinematic moods, squealing dance

On bloody stumps, warlords of delight
In a wreckage of wealth—what we call
A life, is mutilation, loathing, blight:

Original sin made us do it. What's true
Is just what we are. After demonic learning,
In florid cocktail party and petting zoo,
It's time to plan. Will our habit of burning

Light a way to the sea of beauty? Will
Incineration always be a thrill? The fall
Was *such* an idea. Enthusiastic thoughts fill

Us—perfumed, neon vapors of imagination,
Swaggering in tinsel, we curse emancipation.

Getting the Job Done Together

You are not the killer, you say. Death
Does not come from you like breath—

Not from you the bullet in the back
Of stupid heads, slow dismemberment
By dull machete, the dirty burlap sack

Full of body parts, left on the doorstep
Of a worried family. Not from you.
Unless evil feeds on ignorance; unless
In the hidden world, everything you do

Counts: an infinitesimal vanity permits
Poison gas to be shipped. The interment
Of a child, alive, today, elegantly befits

My brief rage at the dinner table tonight.
Indifference is a show of satanic appetite.

Millenniums of Getting What We Want

Do you want respect? To be holy, rich?
Marinated in your own honor? Extinguish

Hope, seek just those rancorous sanities.
Our mind is a jar, our noisy thoughts
So many scorpions striking, inanities

Thrilling to their poison. We gave suicide
Another and a better name. We called it
History. Ignorance was dignity. Ruin, pride.
Our cock-of-the-walk excess, we called it

Victory. Everyone had knives and forks,
We called it culture. The satanic knots
In the gut of time we made, as corks

Were pulled from vintage human poison—
We called it destiny, we called it reason.

Memo From the Study Of the Great Leader

Nothing easier. I can just tell
Who's meant to suffer. I lift the shell—

There they are! I always know where
They are hiding. It is from their fear
I mint my glory. My charm, my care,

Flame-throwing courtesy, smoke of ideas,
Wheel and rack of my worship, all are
Fabulous by their suffering. History says
This is what must be. They cannot bear

Grace. Education breaks their bones.
In this glory, each one is made dear
To us. As they are tied and stoned

Day after day, they show pride and wit.
The rhythm of history: as they get hit.

Good News! A Recipe With You In It!

Beware, that you are not yourself; that
History wants of you what a wildcat

Wants of a deer. Except that humans,
Dear and true, eat each other's souls.
It saves hell the trouble. Their reasons,

Excellent: you are willing to be cooked.
You taste like hatred. The heat brings
Your truth to the table. Have you looked—
To whom do you feed yourself? The wings

You had are the delicacy coveted most.
Your work, your ideas: these are coals.
Your honor and desire they spread on toast.

There is heaven: first and last light given.
But no hell: just you, eaten in oblivion.

O Those Pretty Students

Why a classroom? Not a slaughterhouse?
Every good word crushed like a louse—

A cyanide of ignorance will teach them,
It's a perfect crime: they'll be too stupid
Ever to remember who murdered them.

Make true religion a death certificate.
Everyone proud, virtuous living dead.
If we get 'em early, it's always too late.
They die from what we never said.

We never said: eagles burst from a book
You open with love. A smart girl can kid
Wolves, design mountains. She may look

Inside stars, conduct seasons. Will she live?
And the tigers, the oceans she could give?

And Is There Something Beyond Manners?

Hunger, blood hunger: call it discussion.
They tell us: mood control. No percussion,

Coloratura, whirling tapdance, bear cubs
Interested in nibbling you. No hummingbirds
Who fly in one ear, out the other. No buds

Moist with nectar, touched to the lips
Of a lover. No court jesters permitted!
Be a professional. Do not rise up and tip
Over the day's rum. Use brains outfitted

With oily carbuncles, medals of fatuity.
Master the death-knell of nicety; learn
To be a serial killer using courtesy.

What is trust? What is sunlight worth?
Are there manners of heaven and earth?

An Alternative For the Serial Killer

It would be different, my friend, if you
Thought anything was at stake; if you

Knew you could knock death down
As he stalked a little girl. When
Coyotes will come without a sound

Into your room and let you count
The stars in their eyes; when you,
Easy in revelation, learn the amount
Of mind and soul-stuff created in you—

Then you can be trusted. My friend,
This is the beginning, this is the end,
Paradise is daily. Instead, you pretend

To live. A face shut, praised, laborious.
Serial killer of days, adored, venomous.

A Moment of Reflection at the Office

And so I fail and fail again, my mind
Repulsive in pandemonium. I design

Myself. Virtue is stylish useful darkness—
Greed's sequin. A hidden atom of greed
Destroys a man: in thermonuclear caress

He will vaporize today—heavens move
With just that quick mercy. One speck
Of the laziness that is anger, will prove
A mound of dirt and sewage, to the neck

He is buried, left for carrion-feeders.
One mote of vanity, is the evil seed
Whose flower is torture. We truth-eaters

Will make history. The man, I am the man.
I have gotten all the maggots to understand.

One Man and His Many Close Friends

The bolts that shut the heart, the door
Closed tight on despised flesh, windows
Of learned ruthless eyes—nothing shows
But their own ideas. A golden folklore

Glistening across sandstone, the legends
Of morning light on a palomino mare,
Holy tropical cinnamon indigo air—
All this for them is words. They defend

Personal brute spangled glory, as paradise
Goes off to good whiskey, fantastication
Of summer; to jasmine, trust, tropical ice;
To bread, stone, sex, salt, a delectation

Of soul-bound beauty. These men imagine
Love is about ideas; the world, about them.

But at Least He Was Useful

What of his heart, its tinny clangor
An alarm clock sounding in the house,
Certain to be silenced? A heart like a door
Never in, never out, there for the roust

Of the thief, homecoming of a lover,
Pageant of families, the players who push
Him back and forth, go on to suffer
And to recreate the world; who brush

Him aside. Yet he has a heart—
Like a fireplace. Other people use him
When they are cold, or they need light,
When they are satisfied he goes dim

And returns to darkness, to himself,
Waiting for the fire of someone else.

In Despair at 28, and Looking Around

Gold: loved since it is easily beaten.
History says—try murder to sweeten
The mornings. How can we make a start?
Look: star and acorn in a baby's heart.

You hear bluejays, arrogant with perfection,
Loose raucous and iridescent dreams. We
Could learn a world beyond the confection
We are force-fed; could learn not to be

Practical cannibal of ourselves. We must
Talk to coyotes far in a forest, we should
Practice a jubilance in moonlight, take wood
And whittle a conversation, make trust

Between the cougar and us; on a found planet
Live the peace and preface of our dazzlement.

The North Yuba River Sounds Like

A hum of original creation; sweet hustle
Of air under wings of falcons; rustle,

Then kettledrum of the heart in loving
Rough afternoon sex; white satin
Of the big winds unrolled and moving

Among dragonflies in the grassy canyon;
The calm, sure, urgent, measured, easy
Inevitable come-hither whispers of heaven;
Broken perfect song of anyone gone crazy

Because of beauty; a harmony in the voices
Of a thousand children at play, who begin
To recover all our lost music; the choices

And laughter of the wise, song of reality—
Clear current of living, souls gone free.

Duccio, Simone Martini, Cimabue

Once they painted men and women with a gold
That was the way they lived, in the fold

Between worlds. Around their heads, an arc
That is their own shining, useful, original,
Constant, ordinary, thankful. It is the mark.

It means: nothing can take away their love.
It means: the light in them is permanent. You
Count on them now. From that spirit-trove
Comes everything that exists. What is true

Only. Walk out in the morning. Do you know
Where the light is going? By a seminal
Movement of hours, their story will bestow

Life on life, on life only. Why are you here?
There is gold on earth, and heaven is near.

At Morning on the Coast of Maine

It is sorrow and amusement of the heavens
To watch us with the light that defends

Us each minute against talons of fire
Clawing us with our own thoughts—
With the hot sharp idiocy of desire,

With pitchforks of emotion, knife-edge
Of righteous ideas. Blood is hard around
These tools of history. Yet here, a pledge
Of light, mindful cosmic sugar found

On sweet waters, and rapturous in the eyes
Of our children: this is how the knots
In our hours, our hopes, are all untied

By power, benediction, peace. Shriven—
Could it be so? That we could be forgiven?

Albayzin

We learn that stars live in the mind;
That even now, you are what you find.

We learn how a castle can be made
Of wings, so that stone is weightless
And wild in mystery. In speaking shade

Of our garden, afloat on a soft riptide
Of jasmine, we watch a sidereal show
Bring stories of power to earth. Every crow
Turns white. All the innocents who died

Walk out with their loved ones by a river.
Jacaranda grow out of clouds. The breath
Of a child cools a continent, the grace-giver

That is this city, even now is in creation.
Not even the ashes can avoid revelation.

You're Right, I'm Nothing

I may be nothing, except for the day
I unraveled the rain; except for the day

Golden eagles in a high desert meadow
Gave your children a ride around the sky.
Except for the day a common dirty crow

Flew into your office, landed on your arm,
And dropped a ruby in your hand. I am full
Of sorrow, but someone recalls the charm
Of the salt breeze I called in to cool

Lovers at twilight on a hot Pacific beach.
I am broken. I am the one you despise.
Yet when myriad shooting stars reach

Your house, gather outside your door,
It is you they seek, and you they restore.

Eve Outwits God and Adam

True, Adam named all things of earth.
But he did not love them, not the perch

Of the singing bird nor sunlight coming
Home, and calling us home. But for Eve
Words made beauty. To speak was to sing,

The music a summons; phrase, sentence—
All transparent. She could see through
Them all. Adam's words hard and dense
Walled up paradise. But she was true

To our hopes, because of her we can
Work with mind, because of her we
Make our language a lens. We stand

Here for her. Gods bluster, shove.
Yet, because of her, we can love.

Plato Hitchhiking Around,
Still Can't Pipe Down

The world is made of mind. Material
Has temporary form, dark or sidereal,

Ruined, fabulous, but always borrowed
From a transit of mind—our version,
Project, tool, dream, story, road,

Whimsy, joke, work and delectation, all
Of it for our traveling here, on the way
To another world, and another, that call
Since they are made of mind. We pray

By what we do. We are what we love.
The rest is waste, void, rank perversion.
Celebration below is from fact above.

It means theology is bread. Sky is earth.
Justice beckons. Here is light: search.

Proof of Her Existence

Light. What you do is encoded
In the light. All your life is loaded

Into the light, and sent into space.
The day twenty years ago? The record
Of every idea, fury, touch, and grace

Is on show twenty light-years away.
So that light is not merely miracle,
Lustrous messenger, blessed, workaday;
Light is close, clear, open, mindful.

Your misery, work, what you cherished
Is illuminated. Judged. A raw true record
Is just what she needs. Alive, abreast

Of you, your lies, story, trust, senses:
Light loves you—learn the consequences.

The Speed of Light—No Time, Only Truth

It is not what you say that is recorded,
But what you are. Not facts you sorted,

Hopes, score, presentation, gain, sighs,
Idea, prizes, cakes, dream, phrases
And photos, not your failure, your lies—

But what it meant. So from the sun,
And from every other star, in all galaxies,
By crisscross, signaling, trust and tease
Of light, just there, in that radiant run

Of watchful love, you are inscribed. You
Are there, in your traveling, beyond praises
And beyond all sorrow. What you choose

Within. What you are. Not what you show.
Doom and promise: love, you will know.

A Question For You

What did you do, exactly, to deserve this?
I mean the Pacific Ocean, morning tryst,

Hummingbirds, peach, a spring river tossing
Rainbows. I mean fireflies in the rain forest
Who spell for you the secret word crossing

To heaven, right there, in warm night air.
I mean the first minute you held an infant,
Arms a torrent of diamonds; your ascent,
In dreams, beyond the cadaverous glare

Of history, to a world where you found
A wild elixir of peace. My love, dearest,
How do you live? Where are you bound

If you deserve this? If you deserve this,
Then is all this earth like a first kiss?

Same Old Clarity—Titanic, Ancient, etc.

Pure spring waters rise in the forest,
Rise in the desert, even in the chorus

Of car horns and street talk, in the hum
And hurricane winds of work in the city
You love. In such waters are the sum

Of what we do, clear beauties moving
Irresistibly, inside time. It's why history
Is more than toxic waste, why liberty
Is close to you as blood, why searching

Through all beauties, you will fit
Your soul to destiny. So this clarity
Within your life, is a movement of wit

That is amorous soul. Lose the chaff
You are. Hold heaven. Make her laugh.

El Padrino

You never turned your face away, you
Offered to assist sunlight's projects, you

Thought the heat of summer had ideas
About life; that when morning comes
To unfold the hours again, it's because

It's the chosen way of teaching us all
These centuries how to make a phrase.
You thought that we are here to praise;
That we are here to learn, that the call

Of clarions in history is meant to come
To something. It's curious, the way guns
Misfire around you. Like a noon-time sun

It must be an accident. Histories depend
On your acrobatic peace, beloved friend.

What I Thought As You Talked

A lightning storm in a clear sky, yet
Without thunder, save thunder set

With golden power and soft advent, in
Your words. Clarity, a branching light,
Earthbound irresistible beauties, reason

On wings of playfulness goes to soar,
To dart, search, make a perfect chart
Of essential sunlight; flying far apart,
Yet always present, as you restore

Sound to delicious origins, where ideas
Have a taste, any rock is poetry, sight
Is dream, to say is to love, our tears

Will cure any sickness. You are yourself.
Body amazed, a soul in perfect health.

The Accountant Gets His Wish

It was twilight that visited my room,
Pulled up a chair, talked of the moon—
Her light from fountainhead of reverie,
Gentle trailblazer, my sister in ecstasy.

From books bound with violet petals,
She read; its pages were rare metals
Refined by enchantments that she wrote,
Only twilight can safeguard the smoke

Left when lighting strikes in the heart,
And stars take up places in the chart
Of lovers' hands. There were no regrets
As she took her cloak of stellar velvets,

Looked at me, and to air and light returned—
A woman, the earth: this is what I learned.

If Only She Had More Friends

She learned there is no loneliness like
Company. Solitude is noon, friends night.

Solitary, she knew a tempest, rough winds
And pure voices of the past and future
Blowing through books, as world begins

Again every minute: time and space
Fall in love. Their children are here,
Lovely, shining, mischievous, they dare
You with old condign demanding grace,

Wild studious clowns of the world. How
Can you suffer this solitude, how endure
The milk and honey and loving, the show

Of reality wondrous, there in your room?
How everyone laments your solitary doom.

Sahara Oasis

The heads of date palms—like words
Aloft and at work. The world returns

Here, to say again the names that began
Everything: sun, water, sweetness, stone,
Moon, air, silence. When we understand

We remember, in darkness we must
Listen. What if the oasis means what
We mean? What if beauty is trust
In what does not change, when we let

A world past marry the world to come?
What if body is soul, if we are alone
Only in brutish infidelity; if night musk

Of a beloved holds a desert and the sea?
What if men are women, and you are me?

When Praise Is Fact

It's one thing to make gold from lead.
But the bright gold in what you said,

The way ashes, under your touch, can
Find again improbable fire—you know
Where light travels, you understand

How history's darkness dances in liberty,
How even midnight and ashes are alive,
Infused with your fine laughter, and veracity—
And you, anonymous. Thus, world may thrive—

And no one knows why, no one can
Pester you with admiration. You bestow
Your phrases, and each grain of sand

You hold, is a seed. World, a season.
Your work, a spring river of reason.

Gamble, But Not With History

As a player is dealt a card, so you
Are dealt a self. History hopes you

Will play by the rules of the table.
Stay and bet all your years, even as
You lose them. Intelligent and able,

You think somewhere, someone always
Is winning. Something is just now about
To happen. The excitement! All the days
Brings news, death, everywhere a shout

At victories, thrill, hurt, scrimmage for
Causes, hopes, wealth. My love, have
You forgotten the daily opalescent roar

Outside: words, grass, galaxies, clay?
Take a gamble. Stand. Refuse to play.

Just Before Loving

A tropical afternoon, you on the verandah,
Watching a tangerine crab with violet claw

Made from melted fables; in your face
The trade winds. What is it, love, there
In your touch and musings? A hot grace

Brought by glossy air, by transparent air,
Air ensouled with fragrance, air marked
With amorous message of petals, soft, bare,
Offered in noon light, at midnight; sought

By hummingbirds, bats, acrobatic insects
Painted in heaven and here granted spare
Planetary souls in a forest made perfect

With orchestral nights, wet delicious air,
Your heat and your sweat and lustrous hair.

Costa Rican Rain Forest

Our blood darkens with allspice, legs
Live like roots. Trees are powder-kegs—

Where deep space safeguards stardust.
Here, trade winds compose old music—
Shining become sound. Love and trust

Is only this: all a rainbow of trickery,
Iguana's barroom swagger, insect sonata;
Raucous glass frog, monkey bitchery,
Fashionable pit viper; dolphin regatta

Whose arcs in water match the curve
Of the earth—love, our work is this:
To show how beauty's bright nerve

Brings world together here: agony—
And joy, sex, chocolate, mahogany.

We're Not Alone. We're Not Even Ourselves.

Come home to old hunger, which is
Of body and soul, of a learned kiss

That makes them one, and one the sky,
Grass, summer, winter, word, touch—
In unity is the wisdom where we die

The death we meant. We'll ask death
Into the house, and let him do his
One big trick. So in planetary caress,
With love beyond hunger, we will live

In another world that includes earth
And you, cello and cat, sex and luck,
Oceans and us, galaxies, seagulls. Earth

Bears us, and what we learn to be
Bears us, as one line bears poetry.

She Heads Onto the Open Road

Compatriot, wanderer, my blessing, you
Hold testimony of high desert light, you

Must listen, wherever you go—for there is
Origin and destiny in our subtle country.
Sagebrush will be your sidekick. Give

Away each miracle you are given. And by
Such gifts, have a homecoming of soul
In the bed of this world. You will find
How embraces make diamond of coal:

In heat of lover and beloved, all darkness
Polished to a first, sacramental clarity—
So the days need your touch. Caress

Them, find your way. See life through.
Let world undress the heaven in you.

Life, Death, Dance, and Your Real Face

This is the only day you will live.
Do you think light comes to give

And cannot help itself? Heaven is
A firing squad of luminous offers. You
Must live, laugh, die—this day has

Within it the dancer you could be when
Ancient music in you that might be you
Shines in your flesh. Can world depend
On you, so that hidden work you do

May spin, just now, like a planet—subtle,
Of magisterial bemusements, melodic, true,
A salutary pirouette of everyday? A muscle

That moves soul, gives your body grace.
You are a messenger. Make your own face.

Her Rain Forest in the Winter Storm

Roistering wind, oil-painted sea currents,
Mango trees trussed with fruit, ascents

Of raucous incorrigible parrots: the tropics
In mischief sent this snow. May I inquire
Into your warm beauty? By what tricks

Do you call iridescent heat, trade winds,
This wet simmering, allspice, salt, lime,
The sugar in the air, silence and jasmines
To saturate a morning hour? This rhyme,

My love, this heat, I would match you.
We have matched fidelity with desire,
Frozen drifting mountains with the blue

Astonishment of seas incendiary with coral—
Your pleasures at dawn: tempestuous, floral.

Suppose Love Were Not Just Biology

Take a strand of light, minute bolt,
Set it loose on a meadow: luminous colt

Come home, muscular as an afternoon
In summer. Those hoof beats hold music
That says life, life, life, it says moon

And grass. Ride that colt to your lover,
Find her. Gone off to your skylarking,
In her, with her, together you recover
A way back, a way forward, marking

Night and heart with storytelling sex,
Unity of soul, skin; then the wick
Of flesh lit with a light after death

Of rough spiritous animals, who move
In deliverance of light we can choose.

They Were Expelled, You Led Us Right Back

Your face, in that place just past
The midmost of your pleasure—at last

The bright full fire, delicious truth
Of you, hidden hours of loving all
Brilliant upon you. I see through

This world, by your radiance. I see
Life at liberty, in your wakefulness
Made of moving beauties only. Caress
Is wilderness, your shining is fidelity—

Again you begin to glisten in sweat, you
Taste like peaches, then allspice, salt,
Wayward perfect cream. You come true.

In flamboyant peace, final pardon—
In bed, at home in the first garden.

Maybe You Two Should Be Friends

The still point is the place where
A hurricane grows. A woman's care

Conducts the motion of stars. You
May be nothing, unless what you say
To a lover at dusk calls a blue moon

Over mountains, frangipani on winds
From far tropics to spice you both
On the way to bed. Shining that begins
At night, will summon morning. An oath,

A fidelity at dawn, at whispered birth
Of every word: with sweat you pray.
You have, hold; heaven and earth

Have you, hold life and breath.
Soul on soul—first wine-press.

He Dreams of St. Clare Again

Was it a dream, the house full of light?
Through poverty of soul, we saw delight.

It was a trailer, of painted tin, yet strong
Enough—an outpost on a blue planet
Entrusted with spirit and jokes. Strong

Enough to hold one thousand summers
Of wildflowers to heal our eyes; to have
Stories of power, who visit us with offers
To ride on comets, beyond the sad

Fact of self. This is your home:
A trailer of friends whose contentment
Is firework and first beauty. Go, atone,

Find peace, the plain dream, simplicity—
Women making light, a house of destiny.

The Angel Gabriel Visits a Man in Danger

Straight ahead, the bray, glare, toss
Of everyday. It is distraction and loss.

It is destiny. You strike, you win again,
Remember then how you might answer
Glittering invitations: honor them: send

Them back. The prizes, mincing, drama,
Networking: dear one, it is energetic,
You can make history, can make law;
Yet, forget to take the fat, filthy tick

From inside your heart, and a tract
In oblivion will be yours. The banter
Will pass to other amusements, the rack

Will break one century, another. Let
Heartwork lead to heritage, to the secret.

Primer Found in a Bar

If you would love, understand. If
You would live, stand forth to lift

Hands in thanksgiving. Here is earth.
We must undo darkness with a gift
Found in the canny sidereal church

Of every soul: go there, live there,
Because genesis is today: beginning
Within you. A wild point of care
Is revelation and revelation—all living

Seeks your hands, yours and yours.
Learning is this embrace. The sift
Of heaven and earth together, restores;

What makes light, makes you. In labor,
Beyond sense and idea, a world to savor.

Cook Them, Use Them, Drink Them

Put sentences inside the world, and you
Walk in wilderness, earth unmade, true

And wild with your futures. So then
Begin this humdrum magic you can do
With words: take any handful, dip them

In the sea; bring time reborn in tense
Back with salt grit and a resonance;
Or put each word in a saucepan, dense
With spices. My love, take their sense,

Soak it in rum, blacken it with tar,
Paint it with sweat, run it through
A buzz-saw, a honey-hive. At a bar

Together with friends, brew each word—
Lift a glass of life. Taste, and learn.

Traveling with You, Reader

We saw, in a garden in Spain, an insect
Whose wings were mint, and iridescent

To match the water in a tropical atoll
In the South Pacific. In the Grand Canyon
A rattlesnake on my backpack unfolds

Into beauty, and moves away over rocks
With a perfection of holy winds passing
Over stars. A Sierra sudden in our thoughts
Rises to renew heaven, a granite massing—

Girls climb there, vault to the heavens.
In San Francisco, in a café, an opened
Door in a back wall leads to the reasons

You need to die. Unless you choose to live.
Watch and answer the world, as you give.

The Pest in Pestilence

All virtues come from one: goodness.
All sins—hypocrisy, tedious contest

Of family hate, strut, shout, greed,
Tyranny, tossing of infants into fire—
All from one failure, one seed:

Self-satisfaction. Self is not work,
It is catastrophe: pride, ignorance,
Fear, rape, malignity. The very dirt
Convulses by our disgrace, the dance

Century after century, before the mirror,
Where the one we love most, carnal liar,
Dines on world, knowing himself dear

To history. Would you be whole?
Self annihilated by iridescent soul?

Because of You, Reader

The doors open everywhere, why are
They concealed? The same reason a bar

May serve elixir of life, the very same
Reason sunlight is your first cause,
And passes on with peaceable flame

To a destination of beauties. How does
A song of the world make way through
Our daily clangor of darkness? Because
Of you, reader, because of what is true—

Your hidden comeliness. Because of
What you will do, this world by laws,
In liberty, comes to warn and love;

To beckon. Walk through the old door
To stars. You have been home before.

What We Do in the Great Basin

What if the six days of creation
Are every six days? If education

Holds a genie, a workaday heaven? If heaven
Were more than merely earned—if perfection
Were necessary everyday? And on day seven

In wild country, you give thanks, because
Desert sunlight is rambunctious and in love,
Meteor showers mark you, and sweet laws
For cougar kitten and grizzly bear cub,

For bolt of mustangs at morning, for dust
Dancing with antelopes—a lawful confection
Of all the world is given, shining, on trust.

The unity, pattern, the secret, the revelation—
In one willow leaf is our peace and exultation.

In Your House Watching the Rain

The rain this afternoon is like never
Before. We have been waiting forever

For this, water from heaven that washes
Souls, washes slaughter and humiliation
From history. A sky shows bright arches

Of forgiveness after this storm, we pass
Under them one by one. Now on earth,
We see how we may begin our search,
How to learn to ride the light at last,

How every city is a city on a hill,
How dust is adored, how creation
Is a means of traveling. At the windowsill

You stand; in sight, our cherished land.
Now in every room, a world at hand.

A Friend. Your Friend.

Not books, but what the books mean.
Not world, but heaven earned, unseen.

You open the eyes within your eyes
To see all there is to give away.
You laugh, when you learn the lies

Were your own, and world was hidden
Only because you thought it was yours.
Now you are nothing. Reality pours
From you into this world. You defend

All of us, you fight in beautiful furor
Of wings, yet no one can see the way
You fly on a wind of learning. The door

That is peace opens by your trust—
Opens forever, opens for all of us.

If You Have Eyes, You Can Fly

Beloved reader, when what you do
Is open a soul in your eyes, review

The stagecraft of everyday, your manner
Of traveling, its direction, hope, quality,
Your joke with sunlight: then the banner

Of body and soul will show pawprints
Of wolf pups, perfect form of galaxies
In deep space, stains of peach and dirt,
Ragged sash of rainbow, storm-seas

Headed for a honey of peace. Love, such
A banner, which is yourself, agrees
With an iridescent origin. Live in trust.

Move, world to world, on wings of sight.
Your form flies here, on a wind of light.

The When and Why of Your Wings

Because we must give thanks, that is
Why. Because we are born for a tryst

With world; sunlight slanting through
The lemon tree, and in jasmine flowers
Coming over a wall, archangels who do

Not want you. They want you to love.
Because destiny is making a comeback—
When sandhill cranes gather above
A spring meadow, their mystical track

Glittering in the sky; when in a city
A young woman resplendent in powers
Works at night on a book, and the integrity

Of a better world is burnished; when
With your wings, all the worlds open—

You Knew, You, the Animals, the River, Light

Answers: that's what you are. Every gesture,
Your work, hat-tricks, grammar and temper,

The way night needs your shadow, the way
You salt words you use, before you serve
A sentence to a lover, to heaven; the way

You step outside to serve the light
Of summer and music of rivers. You wash
Dishes and sass the angels; you delight
In comets visiting the earth, so to cash

The checks of heaven, giving to whoever
Gives herself away the gold reserves
Of light, money of soul, now, forever.

You knew how everything is an answer—
You and your loving, you and the panther.

Otherwise, An Ordinary Morning in Granada

It happened one day, for one hour—
Heaven reached down with raucous power,

With a tempest of refinement touched you
And me, neighbors and dogs, grain of sand
And tawny mountain, painted books, kazoo,

The pamphlet with thumbprints of blood,
Grudges flying with their filthy wings
Heart to heart, a dead child in mud,
All this was touched. The brute sum

Of world, its habit of anguish, touched:
For one hour, here in this holy land
There was no hatred. In the land of trust

Our address was Jerusalem. We trusted life.
Every city was Mecca. Each woman, Christ.

Trying to Say How You Are Loved

What if the hand of heaven is open
Always, come to love and defend

You and me and the beauties; what if
When morning light in raucous clarity
Comes to your torment and story with

Movement of first laughter, home-free,
Irresistible—love, what if first and most
That movement means peace. It means
Cherishing. Deliverance. Earth is host,

We are visitors. In hope we are sent
To see if we remember by fidelity
How body is form, light is content.

You will know, love, what you once knew.
You will be light, when light trusts you.

Reader, About this Castle...

In the castle where I work, you will
Find me at door or at windowsill,

Or in a garden with flowers a rainbow
Has soaked in color, or in the kitchen
Of celestial bread, or in the secret glow

Of a room where stars are made by children.
There are stairways to another world, a cellar
With dolphins, a tower whose golden bell
Keeps a time in the mind, and a cauldron

Where the past simmers into perfection,
Tasted by the future. This castle I defend
With sonnets. It is waiting, confection

Of origin and destiny. See love through.
I labor, so your castle is ready for you.

She Confirms with the Angel

Let me get this straight: my spine holds
A geyser that goes from earth to sky, holds

Impulse of lightning bolt and big weather
Of souls waiting for me, the women I will
Become, when I understand? And a feather

From a crow's wing, in my hand, will comb
Darkness from dreams, to leave shining
For my friend a good joke, an idea beguiling
And useful like soil and sunlight, like stone

That is the foundation of the world? I want
To be sure I have this right: rowdy spill
Of the waterfall into my house and thought,

All things possible at once, on earth, as I live?
Furor of paradise in the simplest thing I give?

And You Will Find It

On the other side of light, it is
On the other side of touch, it is

Of the other side of work, it is
On the other side of stars, it is
On the other side of dust, it is

Closer to you than eyes, it is
Closer to you than soul, it is
A road on the map of trust, it is
All a galaxy of exultation, it is

A song within your beauty, it is
Paradise of destiny and origin, it is
Homeland, heartland, memory, it is

More than one life, what you gather
In this light, you and earth together.

Time For You

Time moves because of the movement
In your mind. So everywhere you went

Is with you, waiting for your gift—
Still point, prayer, clarity of words,
Rigor of thankfulness, at last the lift

On wings of understanding, so that you
Can see at once each place you loved.
Then it is that the neon cloudy brew
Of time, with its intoxications, its rub

Against heart and tidal agitations, knock
Of minutes, clangor of melodrama, birds
Writing seasons on sky—then you unlock

The door of space, enter a world of light—
Material soul, first beauty, unitary sight.

As I Was Saying…

Air has senses, sunlight has a memory,
Rivers run into souls, there is prophecy

In commonplace hours. Would you see
Inside this world? Recall how long
World has been watching you. Your liberty

Is there, a raggedy and brilliant chance
To be more than a haggis of desires,
Eaten by history, who sits in a trance
Of hatred. He tastes you now, on fires

Fueled with your deceit. Your only hope
Is air, love, rivers, summer hours strong
By arcana of splendors, learning by rote

The alphabet of stars, as the sky spells
Words that make the story the earth tells.

An Objective Report On You

It is joy, and it is just a beginning.
It is perfection, you are ascending

And it is beginning, you have been patient.
Inside patience is power of lightning.
A music of blessing moves by consent

Of stars, that is a consent you give
At the end, it is the beginning, a joy
Chosen as you laugh and as you live,
Chosen for you, your self you destroy,

This is your joy, to be transparent, as
In the beginning and at the end, wing
Upon wind, because your world has

The love and luck that you make
In the beginning of the end, awake.

Steven Nightingale is the author of two novels, *The Lost Coast* and *The Thirteenth Daughter of the Moon,* and *Cartwheels,* a limited edition book of sonnets, *The Planetary Tambourine* and *Cinnamon Theologies,* **two collections of sonnets** published by the Black Rock Press. A native Nevadan, he received a B.A. at Stanford University where he studied computer science and literature. After living in Spain for three years, he has now resettled in the Santa Cruz mountains near Woodside, California, with his wife Lucy and daughter Gabriella.

COLOPHON

Designed and produced by Bob Blesse at the Black Rock Press, University of Nevada, Reno. The typeface is Dante, designed by Giovanni Mardersteig. The display font is Rialto designed by Giovanni de Faccio and Lui Karner in Austria. Printed and bound by Thomson-Shore, Inc., Dexter, Michigan.